THE

Sales
Strategies

*that will boost
your sales today!*

THE

Sales Strategies

*that will boost
your sales today!*

by
STEPHAN SCHIFFMAN

Adams Media Corporation
Avon, Massachusetts

To Anne, Daniele, and Jennifer

Published by Adams Media, a division of F+W Media, Inc.
57 Littlefield St., Avon, MA 02322 U.S.A.
www.adamsmedia.com
ISBN 13: 978-1-58062-116-8
ISBN 10: 1-58062-116-3

Printed in the United States of America.
J I H

Library of Congress Cataloging-in-Publication Data

Schiffman, Stephan.
The 25 sales strategies for maximum results/ by Stephan Schiffman
p. cm.
ISBN 1-58062-116-3
1. Selling. 2. Sucess in Business. I. Title. I. Title: Twenty-five sales
strategies for maximum results.
HF5438.25.S3334   1999
658.85—dc21   98-31838
CIP

This publication is designed to provide accurate and authoritative information with regard to the subject matter covered. It is sold with the
understanding that the publisher is not engaged in rendering legal,
accounting, or other professional advice. If legal advice or other expert
assistance is required, the services of a competent professional person
should be sought.
— From a *Declaration of Principles* jointly adopted by a Committee of the
American Bar Association and a Committee of Publishers and Associations

This book is available at quantity discounts for bulk purchases.
For information, call 1-800-289-0963

Contents

Acknowledgments

The sales methods you're about to read are the result of many hours of conversation with countless salespeople over the years. My first word of thanks goes out to them.

This book also benefited tremendously from the specific contributions of many people who provided ideas, administrative help, and moral support. I want to thank those people here. To Julie Held, Brandon Toropov, Michele Reisner, Steve Bookbinder, Lynne Einleger, Denise Lopresti, and Sheila Salera, my profound thanks for your support, encouragement, and contributions while I was trying to turn the idea behind this book into a reality.

Introduction

I've worked with a lot of salespeople over the years, and I've also done a lot of thinking about the kinds of sales reps who rise to the top of their profession. I've spent about a quarter century watching and working with these people now, and I think I've reached some important conclusions about them. These salespeople seem to understand a little more about the strategic end of sales than the average salesperson does; they realize that sales is not simply "a numbers game."

Many beginning salespeople approach me during seminars and say, "Steve, isn't sales just numbers? If I make enough calls, follow through enough times, eventually I'm going to make a sale. Right?" Well, yes, but that question ignores a fundamental problem. If you want to have a sales career that's worthy of the name, you have to track more than one number, as my book *Cold Calling Techniques (That Really Work!)* points out. Otherwise, you're basing your life's work on the approximately one-third of sales that are going to come your way no matter what you do. That's not superior sales work!

If sales is any kind of "game," it's a game of ratios. Successful salespeople *begin* their sales work with a thorough understanding of their own ratios, and they develop a deep understanding of the many ways they can *improve* on their ratios—how many dials equal how many contacts equal how many appointments equal how many sales. Improving on those ratios is how superior salespeople excel—and where the ideas in this book can help you.

Successful salespeople know how to find the very best ways to turn strangers into prospects, prospects into appointments, and appointments into customers. They realize that there's more than one phase to the sales cycle, and they keep an eye out for the best ways to maximize their effectiveness during each and every aspect of the unfolding relationship. This book contains some of the best ideas I've encountered over the years for maximizing sales effectiveness throughout the sales process. It will help you improve on your ratios, too.

This book is not the last word on good selling, nor is it a repository for gimmicks you can use to close sales without building up a firm relationship with the prospect. It's meant to be an easy-to-read, easy-to-use resource you can use to increase your competitiveness in short order.

The selling techniques that I've used and taught over the last twenty-five years are simple, direct, conversational, and honest. There are—and can be—no gimmicks within the systems I promote. There's only good, solid relationship-building and a resolute refusal to waste one's time with prospects who aren't likely to buy.

Most sales books still focus on the old objective of "finding the potential customer's need." But that model doesn't work for me. If you needed a product today, you would go out and buy it, whether it be a copier, a long-distance service, life insurance, or anything else. To sell to someone who's already actively in the market simply isn't a big enough goal for success in today's marketplace. Who wants to count on building a career out of sales that fall into your lap? I certainly don't, and I hope you don't either.

The selling model I teach is very different. I define selling as asking people what they do, understanding fully how they do it, when they do it, where they do it, who they do it with, and why they're doing it that way, and then helping them do it better. That's right: Our basic job as salespeople is helping people do whatever they do even better than they were doing it beforehand.

The basic goal is *always* to help people do what they do better—by understanding fully what it is the consumer is trying to accomplish. To do that, we have to ask a lot of intelligent questions based on what the prospect is doing now, has done in the past, or plans to do in the future. That yields better information than focusing in on what we think the prospect needs.

The point of this book is to give you insight into some field-tested, pragmatic methods that will help you do *your* job better. I founded D.E.I. Management Group in 1979, and in the intervening years I've worked with nearly 9,000 different companies and more than half a million salespeople. I've passed along a lot of good information—and I've learned a lot, as well. You're about to learn the key strategies used by salespeople who emerged as top performers in their own organizations. Over the past decade or so, I've made a point of training my own salespeople to use the concepts you're about to discover. They have worked for my people—and for thousands of superior salespeople in the United States and abroad. They can work for you, too.

Good luck!

Take Immediate Action

Not long ago, I was talking with a salesperson about a meeting she'd just conducted with a prospect, a meeting that had gone quite well. I said, "Well, that's excellent. Did you write him an e-mail, thanking him for the time he spent with you?" She said, "No. There's no reason to write him an e-mail to thank him, because I'm going to follow up with him by telephone on Friday."

It was a Tuesday afternoon. What, the salesperson argued, was the point of writing an e-mail? I told her she was making a mistake: there was a very good chance that she would not get through to her contact on Friday—and that whether she did or not, the thank-you note would reinforce her good work during the first meeting. "I'd get that note out immediately," I told her.

Maybe she meant to do as I'd suggested, but the truth is she never sent that note. The two did not connect on Friday. In fact, another whole week went by before she was able to speak with the prospect again. Her sale had stalled; she'd lost momentum. And why? Because she'd decided to "wait to see what he thought of the presentation."

Salespeople must learn to act on what happens immediately. Successful salespeople are constantly asking themselves: "What can I do *now* to move the sales cycle forward?" Too many salespeople count on things unfolding just as the timetable the prospect lays out suggests. I say I'll call you Friday; therefore, I'm probably going to call you Friday. But the reality is, things don't always work that way.

The sad truth is that, early on in our relationship with a prospect, we're not the highest thing on his or her priority list. The information we get is better and the commitments we receive are more meaningful as the relationship progresses and deepens. But at the outset of our business relationship, we don't really know what the other person has in mind. We don't know whether that person will get to talk to the other people in the organization who must sign off on our ideas. We don't know whether the prospect will even read our proposal. We need every advantage we can get. Most salespeople are not quick enough to act on what I consider to be the basic responsibility of good sales work: committing oneself to *move the process forward,* and not relying on others to do so.

In selling, you need to be fast. You need to take responsibility for sizing up the best ways to move the sales cycle forward, and you need to act quickly.

I got a telephone call a number of years ago from a woman who wanted to buy ten of my *Cold Calling Techniques That Really Work* book. It happened to be 10:30 at night on a Friday when she called; I was in the office, working late, so I answered the phone. When I heard that she wanted to order the ten books, I asked myself, "What can I do to move this relationship forward right now?"

So I asked, "What is it you're trying to accomplish? How are you planning to use the books?" To which she said, "I work for a major oil company here in Virginia, and what we're trying to do is get our ten distributors to make more phone calls, and if we do that, we're going to be more effective in our sales." I said to her, "I've got an idea. I'll be in Virginia this coming Tuesday. Why don't we get together?" She said, "You'll come here?" I said, "Absolutely!"

The fact of the matter is my quick action to move the relationship forward led to a $250,000 sale! All this because I chose to take immediate action to find out more about the person, to deepen the relationship, to move the process forward *then and there.*

Most salespeople don't do that. In fact, most salespeople are busy trying to figure out how they can *avoid* having to go on an appointment. They figure maybe they can cut a few corners. My philosophy—and the philosophy of the superior salespeople I've worked with over the years—is very different. *Take action,* and do it now. Get an answer—positive or negative—quickly, and then move on. Reinforce a good meeting *now,* not next week. Follow up a promising lead *now,* not "someday."

For example, recently one of my sales managers ripped out an ad in *Business Week* for a credit corporation and passed it on to a salesperson. The rep made no call on that ad for three weeks. My sales manager, slightly peeved, "repossessed" the ad and called the next day. He got an appointment instantly. We eventually got the business from that ad—but we could have gotten it three weeks earlier than we did. (And that salesperson could have earned a commission!)

Successful salespeople are always thinking about how they can move things forward. They realize that in order to change the status quo, it's usually necessary to act quickly.

Don't overanalyze a situation. Act immediately. Go when the prospect says to go. But also be realistic about what you're going there for—and don't be shy about following up immediately after your appointment, either on paper or by phone. When in doubt, do something that moves the relationship forward!

STRATEGY #2

Take Quiet Time to Think

Most salespeople don't give themselves enough time to think. The successful salespeople I've worked with have usually found ways to build quiet time into their work week—time they use to reflect on where they are, what they're doing, and where they should be going.

It's usually a good idea to find a special place where you can think about your work without being questioned or disturbed. (A salesperson I know recently tried to sit quietly in his own living room so he could think about the challenges he faced in the upcoming week, but family members, unused to his silence, kept walking in and asking him what was the matter with him!)

I love to work on Saturdays, when no one else is in the office, just so I can think. I come in the office, usually about ten o'clock, do some of the paperwork that I have to do, and then think for the next two hours. I don't try to write, necessarily. I go through some papers, review to-do lists, and look at schedules—all of which triggers my imagination and lets me reflect on the work that I'm doing. But I don't interact with other people, and I don't talk. I keep a pad of paper handy so I can write down notes to myself. You deserve some kind of quiet time, too.

Superior salespeople make a habit of analyzing exactly what they are trying to accomplish. They take the time to immerse themselves in their "game plan," reflect on that plan, and look at it from lots of different angles. They ask themselves:

- What am I doing now that's working?
- Why is it working?
- What am I doing now that's not working?
- Why isn't it working?
- What could I be doing differently?

Sales is hard work. It requires persistence, and you do have to make sure you follow through. But you also have to understand what you're trying to accomplish in the first place. Superior salespeople are not robots. They're involved in their own careers, and they make their own decisions. They follow the marketplace trends that affect them. And they make adjustments. Use your quiet time to ask yourself "what's working" questions along the lines of the ones outlined above.

Ask yourself what you can do that will make it easier to achieve your goals. How can you change your selling routine for the better? If you usually make your prospecting calls in the afternoon, what would happen if you made them in the morning, while you're still fresh and enthusiastic? If you usually call the benefits administrator, what would happen if you called the president of the company? What other contacts can you reach out to within your existing accounts?

That last question is a great example of how thinking through new approaches on a regular basis can really boost your income. Most salespeople sell on the horizontal. That is, they sell to the person who bought from them initially. They never really think out ways in which they can escalate their totals by moving on to another person. So they end up selling to the same person who bought a limited amount from them in the first place, and who may lack the authority to buy any additional amount. Such an "upgrade" of your contacts within an organization may require careful planning—but that's what quiet thinking time is for!

We have to take the time to think through our own sales objectives. We also have to take the time to think through the past, present, and future of our prospects and customers. By spending some quiet time with yourself every week (at least), you'll be in a better position to do more of that which does work, and stop doing that which doesn't.

STRATEGY #3

Seize Opportunities

Many salespeople *see* opportunity. Few salespeople *seize* opportunity.

Seizing the opportunity means employing all the techniques possible. It means doing things most other salespeople don't do. Superior salespeople identify opportunities quickly and effectively, and then they use *all* their resources to turn potential success into sales dollars.

What does seizing opportunities look like in action? Let's look at a couple of examples. Consider prospecting, for instance. Most salespeople loathe the process because they don't understand that it's the engine that drives the entire sales process.

There are a number of ways in which you can prospect. One of the most effective is simply by using word of mouth. I make word of mouth work for me by telling every single person I meet what I do for a living. If you were to meet me face to face, I'd tell you that I'm president of D.E.I. Management Group, and that we're a nationwide sales training company with offices in New York, Chicago, Los Angeles, and Dallas. I'd tell you that I have about forty representatives working for us, and I'd tell you some of the companies we work for. Whether we met in a business context or not, you'd get all that information about me and my company when we met.

I'm out to tell everybody what I do because I realize the truth about prospecting: Every single person I meet knows an additional 250 people. And it's a pretty good bet that at least one of those 250 people will be interested in talking to me about sales training at some point.

Understand: I'm not aiming to get you to sign a contract with me when I tell you all about my company. I simply want you to recognize what I do and perhaps tell somebody else about it. I know that every time I tell somebody what I do for a living, I'm probably going to get a lead somewhere down the line as a result of having had that conversation. The best salespeople I've encountered tell everybody in their own circle what they do for a living, and enlighten each new acquaintance, as well. My advice to beginning salespeople is simple: contact all your friends, relatives, and acquaintances and tell them about your business. Don't try to sell to these people—that will turn them off. (My experience is that salespeople who make friends and relatives their primary prospects are not successful.) Simply let these people know what you're doing and describe the way you work.

Other great prospecting tools include cold calling (see my book *Cold Calling Techniques That Really Work!*), giving public speeches (perhaps initially to groups of fifteen or twenty people through a local service organization), or talking to your own accountant or life insurance agent about possible leads you can pursue.

But seizing the opportunity is more than just taking the initiative to track down leads, or even calling several contacts within an organization before you cross it off your prospecting lists. Seizing the opportunity means *taking full advantage of each new situation as it presents itself.* And, paradoxically enough, seizing the opportunity means being able to keep from getting distracted with the idea of closing the sale.

Successful salespeople realize that the phrase "closing a sale" is something of a misnomer. What you're really after is to get people to buy from you—that is, to use your products. Therefore, you have to develop a plan, which we call a proposal, that in fact will show the prospect why he or she should use your product or service. But here's the tricky part: that proposal has to be customized.

The most effective salespeople I know don't use boilerplate proposals. They seize the opportunity to improve the relationship by getting the prospect to develop the proposal with them, step by step, based on the information they've gathered during the interview.

Let the prospect "write" the proposal for you. Ask questions like, "What are you trying to get accomplished in X area?" Then write down everything—and I mean everything— you hear in response. Use your notes to develop a preliminary proposal, one the prospect can sign off on *before* you make your formal proposal. That's a great way to seize opportunity.

Don't wait for the sale to fall into your lap. Don't assume you know the answers. Don't assume that what worked for the last prospect will work for this prospect. Ask the questions. Write down the answers.

Suppose the proposal doesn't go well, despite your best efforts. Seize the opportunity: Use your manager. Have your manager call up and apologize for any problems that might have arisen. (Who knows? You may have said something wrong.) My managers and I have used this technique quite effectively over the years. We'll call up and say, "I understand Jim was out your way recently, and if there was a problem, I really want to apologize." Nine times out of ten the person will say to us, "No, no, no, Jim did nothing wrong. It was just that I was too busy, and I didn't get a chance to talk to my people." And we simply say, "Oh, okay. I'm just curious— what do you do out there?" And suddenly there's a conversation that, more often than you might think, results in new information—and new appointment for the rep who initially called on the account.

Almost as effective is seizing the opportunity by *personally* apologizing for any problems or mistakes in a presentation that didn't result in a sale. In the vast majority of cases, you'll hear, "No, Shari, it wasn't you—we've just got a problem with . . ." All of a sudden you know more about this prospect than you did before, and you're in a better position to act on what you know.

The point is not to simply stare at your call sheet or datebook, not to do what everyone else is doing, but to find creative ways to develop new openings for yourself and gather information about the prospect that you didn't have before. Use all resources at your disposal! That's what seizing opportunity is all about.

STRATEGY #4

Be Punctual

Not long ago, a salesperson came in to see me on a sales call. He was fifteen minutes late. He didn't understand why I was a little bit annoyed at his tardiness. But think about it. Did you ever go to a doctor or dentist who made you wait for twenty minutes—after you'd rushed to get to his office on time? There you are taking a taxicab or driving at breakneck speed in order to get to the dentist for your 4:00 appointment—only to have to spend twenty minutes waiting? That's pretty aggravating, isn't it? My question is: Why on earth should we subject our prospects to those experiences?

A salesperson must be punctual. Period. When a prospect blocks out time to meet with you, you have to move heaven and earth to make the meeting happen at the time you've committed to—and that usually means planning on making your way into the office five or ten minutes before the appointed time.

Treat your own time, and the time of your prospect, with respect. You can do this by:

- Scheduling "hard" appointments ("Yes, I'll meet you at 10:00 on Tuesday morning) around nearby "soft" appointments ("I think we can meet at 1:00, but you'll have to call me to confirm the meeting in the morning.") That way, if your "soft" appointment falls through, you haven't made a trip for no reason.
- Use your off-time (say, 5:30–6:00 P.M.) to compose thank-you letters.
- On those rare occasions when you can't make a scheduled meeting as the result of a dire emergency, call ahead and explain the problem—or try to arrange for a manager or colleague to stand in for you.
- Buy yourself a Day Timer or other personal scheduling aid and use it each and every day.
- Never overbook yourself. If you can't make a certain date and time, say so up

front and schedule your appointment for a date that's not as full.

- Remember who's in charge. If your client needs a few extra minutes to resolve an office crisis before sitting down to meet with you, don't stew about it in the waiting room! Your frustration will show, and will negatively affect the emotional atmosphere of the meeting.

Return Calls within Twenty-Four Hours

I have a policy in my office that none of my calls are screened—and I encourage the sales-people who work for me to follow my example. For the most part, the calls simply come to me: "Mary Smith on line two." As a result, I talk to just about everybody when I'm in the office. I also have all my messages forwarded to me when I'm out of the office. And I return calls within twenty-four hours.

Now, perhaps there's a case to be made that I talk to a lot of people that I don't need to speak to. And yet, every once in a while, there are people who call me because they want my organization to conduct a program for them, people whose names are unfamiliar to me. How can I risk skipping a message or dodging a call when there's a chance that business could be attached to it?

My philosophy, and the philosophy of the most successful salespeople I know, is that you can never afford not to call somebody back—no matter how trivial the call may seem. There's a reason that somebody has called you. The reason may not be what you think it is, but there's a reason why someone has called. Therefore, you really should call that person back, if only to find out what the objective of the call was, and you should find a way to do so within a single business day.

I could give you hundreds of stories of people who have called me up just because they read one of my books and had something (positive or negative) to say about it. And inevitably, when I'm on the phone with someone like that I simply say, "Gee, I'm curious—what do you do for a living?" And in the ensuing conversation I find out more about their businesses, and in some cases, I get opportunities to sell. The point is that by making a commitment to call people back, you find out more about them, and you may uncover new opportunities.

So make the call—while you still have the note, while the question or problem is fresh in your caller's mind, while the "urgency factor" is still working on your side, while you still have a chance to make a good impression. Make no mistake: Returning calls courteously and promptly is probably the single best way to distinguish yourself from the competition in this fast-paced economy of ours. Whether you sell sales training or long distance services or insurance, you want to send the right message: "You're important to me, so important that I'm going to return your call, or see to it that someone else does within twenty-four hours."

Many years ago, I made a sales call to a major communications and technology firm. There in the conference room was a huge poster of the comedian Bob Newhart. His early routines were based on premises that involved his talking to people on the phone. Beneath this huge poster is a caption: "Return your calls, even internal calls, within 24 hours."

Apparently this huge company had a problem: Their people weren't returning telephone calls! Hence the awareness campaign. I decided I was going to make sure we didn't have the same problem at my company. That poster inspired the standard we follow at D.E.I.: Respond to each and every call—and, yes, e-mail messages count as calls—within one business day.

That principle has won us lots of respect, loyalty, and admiration over the years, and it can do the same for you.

Don't put it off! Call back!

See Everyone at Least Once

I feel very strongly about this principle. I believe salespeople should meet, at least once, with everybody who calls in and is willing to set an appointment. By the same token, I also believe that there's no greater time-management sin than continuing to meet, or perpetually attempting to schedule new appointments, with "prospects" who don't represent realistic opportunities for future business.

But first-time appointments? I will make every possible effort to schedule those with anyone who calls me or whom I call—and yes, that includes salespeople who call trying to sell me something. Let me tell you why I think this is an important standard.

You never know where a meeting is going to lead. Remember what I told you earlier—that every person knows 250 other people? At the very least, agreeing to first-time meetings, whether they're with prospects, competitors, or salespeople, puts you in touch with a new network of people.

Recently, a sales rep for an investment firm called me up to ask for an appointment. Not having any reason not to see the person, I said, "Of course I'll see you." Not only did I have the opportunity to hear the person's presentation (a big plus, since evaluating the work of other salespeople is one of my favorite pastimes), but I actually became interested in what this fellow's company had to offer. As it turned out, I became a customer.

At the end of this meeting, I asked the rep, "How did you learn to sell this way? Just how did it come about?" And he started describing a situation with his manager. His manager held weekly meetings, attempting to motivate and train his salespeople.

I called the manager and, without mentioning that I had recently done business with his company, asked for an appointment. The manager was more than happy to meet with me—and I eventually landed a new client for my company!

You really never know who's going to come into your world, and you have to be amenable to the idea of meeting new people. Meet as many people as you possibly can. Commit to a *first meeting*. Just be sure the person knows what you do for a living and knows who you do it for.*

I don't know why so many salespeople are frightened to reach out and meet new contacts, but I do know that those who retain this fear don't move on to become superstars.

Now that it's true, not everybody you're going to see is going to buy from you. Yet, it's also true that, to become truly successful in sales, you have to develop an inquisitiveness about seeing people, meeting people, and understanding what's happening in their lives and in their businesses. You can't be afraid to ask, "Hey, why don't we get together Tuesday at 10:00 A.M.?" And you can't be afraid to say, "Sure, I'm free for lunch on Thursday. Come on in. Let's chat."

What's the worst thing that can happen? You can identify a mismatch. That's really no problem. You just move on. But at the very

---

* In many selling situations, managers decide to ask their reps to focus on setting first appointments with particular kinds of decision makers. That's fine—as long as you remember that having *some* contact with a large potential customer is better than having *no* contact.

least you've passed along a business card, learned a little more about the world you live in, and maybe, just maybe, picked up some more information about the ways you should—and shouldn't—try to sell to other people. And you might just have a good time in the process.

STRATEGY #7

Know When to Retreat

Recently, I was in California working with one of my sales representatives; we were talking about a prospect that he had been working with for the last four or five weeks. He'd gone to the prospect's office, gotten his information together, and made a good, solid proposal. In fact, his proposal was so good that I thought it really did make sense for us to do business with this company.

When I accompanied my rep on his third sales call to this company, I said to the prospect, "Bob, I really believe this proposal makes sense and we should go ahead." Bob was extremely interested in what we had to say, and he, too, felt it made sense. The only problem was that there were a couple of minor issues that still needed to be resolved;

we would have to return with a more specific, revised proposal.

Things looked good until my sales rep called again the following week and could not get Bob on the phone. After three attempts to get a return call, he called me up and said, "Steve, can you call Bob and see if you can get him on the phone?" I called once but didn't get him on the phone. Eventually, it became quite obvious that Bob did not want to return our calls. And the sale, for now, was dead.

So what's the lesson to be learned? There are times when it makes sense to retreat and not waste any more of your time pursuing a prospect. (In this case, that time came around the fifth unreturned call, although an argument could be made that it could even have come a little sooner.) Sometimes you're just not the right person to make the sale, and sometimes it's not going to happen, no matter how good you think you are and no matter how much sense it seems to make for you and the prospect to do business together. Sometimes you do the very best you can and it's pretty darned good, and things still don't work out.

Unfortunately, a lot of salespeople continue making calls well *after* this point of honorable retreat has passed. They continue going back to the same prospect week after week. I was up in Canada not long ago, working with a major telecommunications company there, and I noticed that the pages of most of the salespeople's notebooks were dog-eared. Each page had a profile on a different prospect. These reps were simply calling the same prospects—prospects who had repeatedly rejected them—over and over again! Where on earth, I thought to myself, was the new business supposed to come from?

I've talked to many salespeople who tell me that they make a hundred cold calls a day. In fact, what they do is call ten familiar people ten times a day. That may add up to a hundred *somethings,* but it's not a hundred cold calls in my book. I once ran into a sales rep who swore up and down that she had called someone 437 times in a vain attempt to get an appointment. I don't know whether or not I believe the part about the number of calls, but I do believe she never managed to schedule the appointment. The poor prospect must have dreaded the idea of developing a long-term business relationship with this person!

It's important to understand that some prospects will say "no" to you *by never saying anything.* You have to realize when you're getting that message and be willing to move on. In Bob's case, he'd really left us a message even though he hadn't left us a message. That is, his refusal to return the calls really was telling us something. He wasn't interested in doing business with us. So what's the point of going back and calling him over and over again? That's a game that far too often turns into an adversarial situation. The unspoken message: "You'd better call me back quick—because I want an explanation about why you haven't returned my last seventeen phone calls." How likely is it that you'll want to launch a business relationship that starts out like that?

In some cases, there really is nothing we can do to turn the situation around. Not many sales trainers will admit this openly, but in the real world, it's quite common to run into situations where your best and most appropriate response is to *leave the prospect alone and spend your time in a more efficient way* (i.e., call someone else). When you run into someone like Bob—someone who decides to simply drop out of the relationship—don't play ego games. Let it go. Forget it. Pass. Leave it alone. Move on.

Sometimes the chemistry simply doesn't click; sometimes you have no control whatsoever over the reason someone decides not to do business with you. Maybe you're too tall or too short or too redheaded or too something else that turns this person off. *Find someone else to talk to*—don't take it personally. You can't make a trusting business relationship happen by sheer force of will—it's a consensual dance between two people. If one of the people doesn't feel right about the way something's going, there's no point in pressing the matter.

Years ago, my two daughters had two gerbils. Both gerbils ran around in that little wheel that we got them. At night they would go around and around and around, and they were exhausted during the day even though they went really no place at night. We call that "gerbil salesmanship." I've talked about that kind of sales work in many of my seminars. Some salespeople go around and around and around, never getting ahead. All they manage to do is tick off someone— someone who might have represented a prospect at some point in the future, but now won't, because of the "curse of the gerbil."

It happens to everyone. Major sales seem within our reach and then, for unfathomable reasons, they collapse. If you know when to walk away, you still have the chance to do business with that prospect at some point in the future. If you *don't* know when to walk away, but insist on badgering your prospect until he gets anxious when he hears your name or your company's name, then beware: You've just inherited the curse of the gerbil. This prospect, and this company, will, in all likelihood, never do business with you.

Think in the long term, and remember that "retreat" doesn't mean "defeat." Twelve years ago, I tried to sell our sales training services to a major New York bank, but the bank president looked me in the eye and said to me, "Look, let me put this as plainly as I can: we'll never hire people like you. We don't want to have the kind of culture you represent. Thank you very much." Talk about a crash and burn! And yet, about three months ago, I conducted the first of a series of training programs for that bank.

Time passes, things change. Don't be too concerned about temporary setbacks. Keep your eyes on your job, don't play head games, do your best, and you will, eventually, get business from a lot of the people who once didn't give you business. I promise. In the meantime, learn when to back off.

There's a difference between being persistent and being obnoxiously persistent.

Sometimes the best and most effective brand of persistence is that which allows you to dis-engage for a while and see what happens. Make sure you're on the right side of the line—and make sure you don't waste your precious time on prospects who've already taken themselves out of your cycle.

We will all lose battles. The objective is not to avoid losing a single battle, but to win the war. When it's time to retreat, pick up the phone and start prospecting so you can build a business relationship with someone new.

Know When to Ask for Help

Successful salespeople understand the need to ask for help. They're not at all shy about seeking it out.

At a seminar not long ago, a woman came up to me and said that she was going to go to her manager to ask for some help in securing a sale. But she had misgivings. She said to me, "Doesn't it make me look weak if I can't close a sale by myself?" To which I replied, "No. Absolutely not. In fact, if anything, it actually makes you look stronger."

Salespeople who know how to say, "Help me out here"—to customers, prospects, or their own superiors—are, in my experience, usually among the very top performers in their organizations. Let's look briefly at the different types of help you can get.

Appealing for help can mean simply *letting the customer correct you.* Superior salespeople know that when the customer corrects them, everyone wins. The best salespeople know how to elicit "corrections" that improve the relationship—and raise the quality of the information the salesperson gathers.

Let me give you an example. One of the techniques that we use at D.E.I. is the concept of an outline. What we will do is sit down and have an initial meeting with a prospect and then go through some of the basic steps of our sale. We'll explain a little bit about what we do and how we do it. We'll also find out what they do, how they do it, when they do it, where they do it, who they're doing it with, and why they're doing it that way. But we *won't* try to close the sale at that point, nor will we follow up immediately with a formal outline. We'll find a way to get the customer to correct us.

I rarely come back with a formal proposal on the second meeting, and I may not even get to the formal proposal by the third meeting. Instead, what I do is say to the prospect, "Let me think about what you and I have said. Let me put down some notes and what

I will do is come back next week—say, Tuesday, at 10:00? Let me come back next week, and then I'll go through all the assumptions at that time."

What happens the following week? When I go through the various assumptions of the preliminary proposal, the prospect is either going to tell me that I'm right—or that I'm wrong. If I'm wrong, then by definition the prospect is offering meaningful feedback. He or she is telling me, "No, Steve. Here are the assumptions that you made that are wrong. And here are the correct assumptions." I know where I stand. I've been corrected. My formal proposal avoids some big problems.

At a recent presentation before the board of directors of a Fortune 1000 corporation, my salespeople and I went through five assumptions that we had picked up from our initial conversation. Four of them were correct. The fifth, for some reason, we got wrong. Now I don't mean to say that it was totally wrong, and in thinking about it in retrospect, I realized that our contact might have actually given us some different information the first time than he did the second time. That's the way it works in sales—people get more direct with you as the relationship between the two companies becomes more important to them.

What mattered wasn't whether we were misled during our initial meeting, but the fact that, in the subsequent meeting, we worked toward the common goal getting the proper answer for this company. We got the help we needed from our prospect, and we ended up getting the sale.

You can also seek help *from your managers and peers.* I encourage my salespeople to make sure they call and advise me as to the next step they're taking with a prospect after their initial meeting. If they need me or one of the other executives in the company to come along, then we talk about that. I try to make sure this kind of help is restricted to second, third, or fourth meetings with key prospects. (The first meeting really isn't the big deal so many salespeople assume. Think about it. Lots of people will agree to see you initially, but far fewer will commit to a date and time for that second meeting.)

The odds are that you know people who know your product or service a lot better than you do. They're technical experts. Are you using those experts effectively to get the additional information you need to make a customized presentation? For example, are you saying to the prospect, "Here's an idea. Let me bring back the technical expert next week. Instead of me simply coming back and trying to explain this, let's let you talk to Tammi; she's really is an expert in that area. I'd like her to meet you." You may even be able to get *your* technical expert hooked up with the *prospect's* technical expert. That escalates the sale and gets more people involved in the process, which is usually a good sign.

For crucial meetings with important prospects, it can often be a big help to get your sales manager—or, perhaps even more important, one of your company's technical people—to accompany you on a visit. So feel free to ask. That's what the superstars do!

Know How to Develop Interdependent Relationships

Successful salespeople realize that their work is about relationships.

There are actually four levels that each of us go through when we're selling. The first level is that of the seller, meaning that we're (for lack of a better word) peddlers. Now that's the lowest common denominator that I can think of when I describe a salesperson: a peddler. We come in and we only talk about dollars (or instant delivery, or some other topic of instant and immediate interest to the prospect). We close the sale on one factor that is of deep interest to our customers. There's only the vaguest hint of a real relationship with the customer. Everything is set up for the short term. We don't really expect this connection to last for long. We may have the best price—for now—but we're incredibly vulnerable to competitors, and the moment a better price (or a faster turnaround or a better service plan) comes along, we're almost certainly going to lose a customer.

The second level is that of the supplier. A supplier is typically somebody from whom a customer buys something on an ongoing basis. We're still vulnerable to shifts, but perhaps not as vulnerable as we were when we were a seller. We've got a little bit more information about what the prospect is doing, but we still don't know all that much about his or her business.

The third level is that of the vendor. The name "vendor" implies loyalty, trust, and a deepening relationship. The aspect of trust is important: the customer trusts you, you understand the customer. You've come through on a number of different levels. You're not going to wake up to learn that you're no longer selling to this customer. If there's a sudden strategic change, you're going to have some advance warning, and probably a chance to establish the relationship on a new footing.

Most salespeople tend to be either sellers or suppliers. A minority work their way into the third level, that of the vendor. But highly successful salespeople move on to a fourth level. They become partners.

Highly successful salespeople work for months and years to develop relationships with customers that are interdependent and mutually beneficial—not unlike a marriage. As in any good marriage, both partners need each other, and there's a shared planning process. If you track down as much information as you can about the company you're selling to, if you learn as much about its challenges and goals as some of the senior people at that company, if you consistently develop ways that help these people do what they do better, if your contacts routinely request your input before making major strategic decisions, then you're a lot more than just a salesperson. You're a partner.

For the last twelve years I've been working with a major company, and every single November we plan out the next year's activity—not just what kind of seminars I'm planning to offer, but how those seminars and training sessions can best support the company's most important emerging objectives.

That's partnership. That's the ideal situation. That's the payoff for asking the right questions over a long period of time—and working with your contact to find the best ways to help his or her organization do what it does better. Your goal is a relationship in which you and the customer depend on each other in a partnership relationship.

Sales is fundamentally dependent upon other people, but it's only when we reach the partnership phase that we realize the many benefits of this dependency. There are a million things you can do by yourself, but there is really nothing about success in sales that can be traced to anything you do by yourself. Sales is a dependent activity. The better you work with and interact with other people, the more successful you're likely to be.

Sales, then, is all about relationships. Superior salespeople learn how to build those relationships properly.

A lot of salespeople confuse relationships with time. Don't be one of them. The fact that I spend a lot of time with you does not mean that I have a great relationship with you. (You could be, for instance, looking for a way to justify your presence on the staff; maybe scheduling lots of meetings with lots of salespeople is the way you accomplish that. I've met plenty of people who fall into this category!)

Relationships aren't static; they're interdependent and dynamic. Having a real relationship with a prospect or customer is the same thing as being part of the planning process... and moving toward that partnership role.

Know When Not to Be Dependent

Here, I'm talking about avoiding the trap of believing that someone other than you can assume responsibility for building and maintaing relationships with your prospects and customers.

I'm often criticized because I believe that a sales manager's only function in life is to make sure that you get paid—that is, to see that you get your full commission and, occasionally, to accompany you on sales calls. (Their presence can serve as a signal of how important the prospect is to your organization.) Sales managers do not, however, show up in the morning to make sales—and despite what some in your organization may think, they cannot motivate the salespeople who report to them.

Both of those jobs, selling to prospects and customers and keeping yourself motivated, are yours and yours alone. Depending on sales managers to establish final terms with the prospect is not the kind of help for which you should appeal. If you're not taking responsibility for the relationship with your customer, then you're not doing your job as a salesperson. And if you look to someone else to motivate you on a daily basis, then you're definitely not doing your job as a salesperson.

Fortunately, the very fact that you're reading these words means that you're already ahead of the game when it comes to taking responsibility for key aspects of your job as a salesperson. Ninety percent of all salespeople in the United States fail to read a sales book during the course of a given year!

How can you continue the good work and take full responsibility for your own motivation and your relationships with your prospects and customers? Here are some of the steps the highly successful salespeople I've worked with have taken.

- *Get organized.* Set up a priority list that allows you to focus on the most important objectives each day, and review that list regularily.
- *Focus on the best prospects first.* Divide your active prospects into A, B, and C categories—and make sure you spend the majority of your time with the prospects who represent the "best bets." *Don't* simply call your list in the order in which the cards happen to be stacked on the desk!
- *Develop a regular prospecting routine.* Instead, they don't have enough prospects in the pipeline at any given moment to account for the natural erosion of prospects (which occurs any time you sell something!). Instead, they prospect in a hit-or-miss fashion, when they can't think of anything better to do. Successful salespeople, on the other hand, prospect for new business daily—typically for at least an hour a day.
- *Write e-mails and make calls.* I've already dealt with this briefly in Strategy #1, but there are many more applications to consider. Take responsibility for relationships—thank the new people on

your calendar for taking the time to see you, and thank current customers for their business. In addition, you should occasionally call or drop a line to contacts you haven't heard from in a while.

Don't expect the higher-ups in your organization to let your customers know how much their business means to you. Do it yourself! You won't regret doing so. Recently, I called thirty-five of the people who had played a major role in giving my company business in the last quarter. I simply thanked them for the business. Out of those thirty-five calls, nine people called me back specifically to give me additional business for the next quarter! That's a high-impact calling campaign if there ever was one.

Know when *not* to be dependent! You can't expect anyone else to manage your sales career for you. You have to do it yourself, one day at a time. I believe that every morning, of their own initiative, salespeople should adopt the slogan of the legendary Hollywood agent Swifty Lazar: "Make Something Happen Before Lunch."

Consider Yourself to Be a Messenger of Change

There's a point in my seminars when I ask salespeople, "Who's your number one competitor?" Of course, they name every company they can think of that's offering a similar product or service. And they're all wrong. The number one competitor every single company faces is the status quo. What the prospect is *already doing* is your competition!

As we've seen, the key objective of selling is asking people what they do, how they do it, when they do it, where they do it, who they do it with, and why they're doing it that way. And then our job is to help them do it better. But in order to help them do it better we actually have to become messengers of positive change. Successful salespeople are prepared to do that, day in and day out.

In order to be successful at selling, you're going to have to get someone to change what he's doing now, to work with you instead of following the path of least resistance. Are you ready for that?

How do you pull something like that off? First and foremost, you have to know your own product or service very well. (In other words, you have to be comfortable actually using it, just as a customer would.) Number two, you have to be convinced, deep down, no kidding, that your product will, in fact, help people. And finally, you have to be versatile enough to adapt your product or service to whatever it is the customer is trying to do. This assumes, of course, that you're willing and able to listen to the customer long enough to find out what he or she is trying to do!

Not long ago, I was teaching a course in a high school about sales. (Yes, believe it or not, there are people in high school who are interested in careers in sales!) As part of our giveback to the community, we do work with high school students in New York City; at the conclusion of one class, I was asking the students to tell me what they'd picked up from this initial discussion that we'd had about sales. One young man raised his hand and said to me, "Mr. Schiffman, the one thing that I've learned today is that you aren't as important as what the customer is all about; you have to say to yourself, 'The customer is really more important to me than anything else.' And what it is they want to do, what they are trying to accomplish, and how they want to do that is much more important than your product or anything that you have to say."

He was absolutely right. A superior sales person has to accept that: There's no lecturing prospects or customers, no reading from brochures, no memorized monologues. None of that is as important as asking, "Hey, what are you trying to get accomplished here?" and then listening for the answer that comes our way. Once we hear that answer, once we can respond intelligently with suggestions based on our own product knowledge, then we're in a position to help bring about positive change. Not beforehand!

STRATEGY #12

Evaluate Effectively

It's been said that 90 percent of the things we worry about never happen, and that five percent of the things we worry about are things that we can't do anything about. That leaves us spending 95 percent of our worrying time focusing on the wrong things!

Superior salespeople know how to distinguish important or critical problems from mundane ones. I had someone tell me the other day that she was trying to make a sale that she'd been working on for nearly three months. The sale was worth about $50 a month. She had gone back seven times to see this individual. Other prospects on her list represented roughly eight to ten times as much money as this one did.

I asked her, "Why are you doing that? Why are you going back to talk to this person?" She said, "Well, Steve, it really isn't the sale any more, it's the challenge. It's the challenge of making the sale."

That kind of challenge is too expensive!

Many, many salespeople worry about the wrong things. "What if the person says this, or what if the person says that?" Who cares? Make the call and see what happens. If you've been selling for a month or more, you've made enough sales calls in your career to realize that they're not all *that* different from one another.

Plenty of salespeople get so worked up about what *might* happen during a sales call or an appointment that they overprepare—and then get completely flummoxed when the prospect or customer doesn't follow the script! Then there are salespeople who get so terrified of their encounters with a customer or prospect that they go to great lengths to "make contact"—for instance, by leaving messages—but would really prefer not to interact with the prospect at all!

Why, you ask yourself, would anybody bother to do that? I don't have the answer, but I will tell you that any number of salespeople will go through some amazing routines to reach out to prospects they don't really want to talk to. If that's not a waste of time, I don't know what is. Recently I had someone come into my office, and after sitting and discussing with me what he wanted he wanted to sell me, he said, "Mr. Schiffman, what I would like to do is prepare a proposal for you. But I don't want to take your time. I'll just drop it off and you can give me a call." Those were his actual words. I stared at him and said, "Why would you want to do that? Why would you want to go to the trouble of preparing a proposal specifically for me and then drop it off and let me make the decision of whether or not to make the next call—which I may or may not do? What if I have questions about the proposal?" He said, "Well, Mr. Schiffman, you're busy and I don't want to interrupt what you do."

Well, that's precisely what you're doing when you're a salesperson. *You're interrupting what I do* because you feel that you can help me do what I do better. You can do that only by setting priorities, listening to me talk about my operation, and, eventually, suggesting what I ought to do next!

Superior salespeople don't apologize for that process, or fret endlessly about its possible ramifications. They know when they stand a good chance of adding value to someone's day and when they don't. They don't worry about things they can't control. They simply make the best evaluations they can, and then act accordingly.

STRATEGY #13

Observe

Recently I did a training program with a company in Los Angeles. Part of my presentation involved challenging the sales reps to find new opportunities for business—material for prospecting that no one in the organization had taken advantage of up to that point. Most of the salespeople I was working with were skeptical. "We've already pretty much done it all," they told me. "There are no new companies to call."

Well, if there's one thing I've learned over the past twenty-five years, it's that there's always an opportunity for new business if you're observant enough to look for it. During a break, I picked up a copy of the *Los Angeles Times* and I went through the paper— the business section, the classified section, the wedding section, the obituary section, every section I could think of—and circled every company that seemed like a possible match for the organization I was training.

As it turned out, I came up with 198 different companies that these sales reps had never contacted before. That's one newspaper, in one day. All of a sudden, there was some new prospecting for these salespeople to work on!

If we're motivated to observe—if we ceaselessly ask ourselves, "What's new about this situation? What can I use to my advantage that I've never seen before?"—then we observe. We find ourselves wondering, "Hey, what do you think I might be able to find in that newspaper this morning?"

In my experience, superior salespeople are superior observers.

Part of observing is being open to new ways of doing things. I've already mentioned the power of reaching out to new prospects by giving speeches and mentioning what you do to your friends, relatives, and acquaintances. Maybe, for you, observing means taking advantage of new opportunities in these areas. (Please note that reaching out via public speaking isn't anywhere near as scary as it sounds, and it can deliver some extraordinary new leads for your sales work.

After a recent speech, I walked away with seventy-five new business cards from new acquaintances!)

The point is that you should always be on the lookout for new opportunities for business, whether that means introducing yourself to everyone in sight after a speech or professional function, or mailing a round of letters to customers and prospects, or taking a marker to your Sunday paper to identify new business opportunities. Keep an open eye— even when you're off duty!

Many of my best sales reps carry small pads of paper with them at all times—weekdays, weekends, whenever—exclusively for the purpose of jotting down names of companies they notice. Perhaps they pass a billboard, or see an ad on television, or notice an article in the newspaper. Later, they call their "pad companies" and try to set up appointments. If you make a habit of being observant in this way, then you'll never fall into the trap of believing that there's no one new to call. (See also Strategy #23, on making the most of fallback opportunities.)

STRATEGY #14

Ask the Right Questions

Let's suppose you walk into my office and you notice that I've got a large brown cow in front of my desk.

You don't know why there's a cow in my office, but there is. Not a picture of a cow or a statue of a cow, mind you, but a real, live, big, brown cow. I notice you looking at the cow and I mention that I've had the cow in my office for the past two years. Now, right off the bat, you don't know anything more about why this cow has taken up residence across from my desk for that period of time, but you do know one thing: having this cow on the premises *makes sense to me for some reason.*

If having a cow in my office *didn't* make sense to me, what would I have done? Gotten rid of it!

So why would I have a cow in my office? Let's think about some of the reasons. Maybe I like fresh milk; maybe I find the sight of the cow relaxing; maybe I like the "moo" sound it makes from time to time. Whatever reason I've chosen, though, you know that it makes sense to me.

So let's assume that you sell cows for a living. And let's assume that you don't know which of the reasons we looked at is the one that best describes the reason I've got that cow in my office. Before you start talking to me about how great your cows are, what kinds of questions should you be asking me?

The successful salesperson will ask question like these:

- Why a cow?
- How did you get that cow?
- How did you decide to put a cow in your office?

The mediocre salesperson will ask a question like this:

- What don't you like about that cow?

If I didn't like the cow, I would have gotten rid of it already! Other dumb questions include: "What *do* you like about that cow?" And *some* mediocre salespeople won't even bother asking anything at all. They'll just unfold a brochure about the type of cow they sell, smile, and read it, word for word, to the other person while the cow the person selected is sitting there, chewing away at the carpet earnestly.

"Gee, I notice there's a big cow in the middle of your office."

"Yep. I had that cow shipped in here about three months ago."

"Hey, that's great. You know, our cow gives more milk than the cow you've currently got in your office!"

What if I'm lactose intolerant? What if my cow is there to relax me? Or to serve as a conversation piece? Or to impress an important client who visits me regularly and has a mania for taking pictures of cows? All that talk about milk won't make any difference to me!

Unsuccessful salespeople don't ask meaningful questions, or don't ask questions at all. They engage in what I call "slapshot" selling. They try to close from the moment they walk in the door, and they respond to virtually everything the prospect says with some variation of, "Hey, we've got just what you need," even though they know virtually nothing about what the prospect does.

The slapshot selling model looks like this:

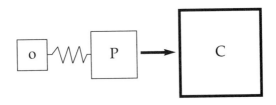

The "O" stands for "Opening." The "P" stands for "Present." and the "C" stands for "Close." Notice how big that C is. Mediocre sales reps spend a huge amount of their time trying to close sales in the slapshot model. They introduce themselves, they may bat a few questions around, and then they try to be present so they can move in for the close. "We can do that too, we can do that even better, in fact. Why don't we set you up with . . . ."

As abrasive as it is, and as uncomfortable as it makes the vast majority of prospects who encounter it, the slapshot model *will* result in sales sometimes. But the slapshot model won't deliver as many sales as you deserve.

Here's the model we use—the model our people have been trained to work from instead, the model that's just about as far from Always Be Closing as it's possible to be.

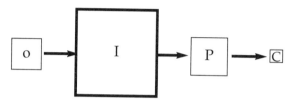

There are four phases to this cycle. The first thing you probably noticed was that the biggest element is not the closing phase. (Let me add, as a side note and for the sake of accuracy, that I'm not crazy about the term "closing." I prefer to think of formalizing the deal as the prospect's simply "using" what we have to offer. But most salespeople are used to talking about closing sales, so we'll hold on to that terminology.)

Note that the biggest element of this sales model is the interviewing stage. That's where you find out why the person's using the cow.

By contrast, everything else in the cycle takes up very little time. There's an initial opening, or qualifying phase, which leads to the all-important interview phase. Then there's the presentation phase, which is the second largest element, but still significantly smaller than the interviewing phase. And finally, there's the closing phase. If the previous three steps have been carried out correctly, closing is a tiny dot, a simple question that lets us confirm that the prospect is ready to formalize doing business with us. (See Strategy #25, Keep the Closing Phase Simple.)

The whole cycle is driven by your willingness to *ask questions*—about the past, the present, and the future—and thereby move the sales process forward.

- Gee, what made you decide to put a cow in your office?
- How long have you been using live cows as a stress management tool?
- How did you decide that stress management is important to your organization?
- Have you ever considered using other types of stress management tools?
- Which ones?
- Why did you choose that kind of stress management tool before you put the cow in here?
- What happened when you tried to take that approach?

- What other stress reduction strategies have you been considering for your employees?

Sales reps who don't ask questions but assume from the get-go that they know exactly why the cow is sitting in the office aren't the kinds of salespeople who emerge as superstars. Sales reps who admit that they *don't* have all the answers ask lots of questions about the past, the present, and the future—in addition to appropriate how and why questions—and they are likely to be highly successful.

Always Try to Move the Sale to the Next Step

As we just learned, there are four phases in the sales cycle. When I give seminars, I always outline those four steps for the audience, and then I ask them, "What's the objective of the first phase?" And inevitably people say things like:

"The objective is to get the order."
"The objective is to meet the person face to face."
"The objective is to understand the customer."
"The objective is to ask questions."
"The objective is to close the sale."

"The objective is to establish rapport."

"The objective is to plant the seeds for a future relationship."

All of these answers are common. And all of them are wrong.

The objective of each phase in the model sales cycle is always to move ahead to the next phase. When you're opening, the objective is to get the prospect to agree to move forward into a meaningful interview phase. (We call this kind of assent "playing ball.") When prospects are in the interview phase, the objective is to get the prospect to help you track down the information necessary to develop a presentation that fits the prospect like a glove. (That's the longest part of the whole process.) When you're in the presentation phase, the objective is to conduct it so well that the prospect agrees to become a customer when you say, "It makes sense to me—what do you think?" (That question, of course, marks the fourth and final phase.)

Recently I was running a training program at a major investment house, a company that sells to customers known as very high net worth individuals. I sat down with one salesperson and had an interesting discussion. He was explaining how well he had done in a meeting with one particular high net worth individual. I asked, "When are you going back to see the person?" because the strategy is to return to see the person. He said, "Steve, I've got that under control." I said, "That's great! What are you going to do?" He said, "Well, I have to get information from her first, that is, I have to get her statements from her other investment house. And as soon as I get that, then I'm going to go back and make my appointment. So I feel pretty secure about that."

I said, "That's fine. By the way, did you give her the special envelope, so she can send back the information, or so you can pick it up when it's ready?" He said, "Well, no, I haven't done that yet. I haven't even thought about that." I said, "Well, let me ask you a question. Did you talk to her assistant? After all, here's a person making, what, ten million dollars a year? She must rely pretty heavily on her assistant to keep track of everything. Did you mention to the assistant that you'll be back when the statements are in?" "Well, no. I didn't do that either." Then I asked, "When do monthly statements typically come in?" "Usually during the first week of the month." There was a long pause. This conversation was taking place on the *twelfth* of the month.

I said, "So what are you doing now?" He said, "I'm waiting for this person to call me. You know, it's a little late in the month, but she'll call. I'm sure she will. She told me she would call."

She didn't call. She never called. He never got that sale.

At D.E.I., our definition of a prospect is somebody who's playing ball with you. A prospect is somebody who is going to answer your questions. Ask yourself: Who answers questions about the large brown cow? Who answers questions about coming back? Who answers questions about what they're doing and how they're doing it, when they're doing it? If you can't get a commitment for a specific next step of some kind, either on your part or the other person's, then you're not dealing with a prospect.

So what strategy can you use to advance the sale? The first and most important one is *always ask for the next appointment at the conclusion of a face-to-face meeting.* No matter who you are, no matter where you are, no matter when you're seeing the person, ask for the next appointment. Now inevitably people say, "Well, Steve, it's a bad time to ask for an appointment. It's just before the holidays, just after the holidays, just before the summer, just after the summer, just before the winter, or just after the winter." They give a million reasons they can't ask for the next appointment. I can only tell you one reason you should: To find whether or not the person is interested in playing ball with you. If you run into someone for whom it's *always* a bad time, there's a problem somewhere.

Successful salespeople move the sales process forward, and they typically do this by closing each meeting with a request for a specific appointment for the *next* meeting. Some salespeople say, "Steve, how can I ask for an appointment? I've got no reason to come back yet!" Sure you do! Here's what my own top performing sales reps say at the end of their appointments: "Mr. Prospect, I have an idea. What I'd like to do, instead of ending right now, is think about everything you've told me and look over all the notes I've taken today. And over the next week, I'm going to put together an outline of what we might be able to do for you, and I'd like to come back in a week and show you what our thinking is."

At that point, you are in essence throwing the ball out to the contact. (You'd be doing the same thing if you asked the prospect to meet with one of your technical people the following week to discuss the issues that have come up during your first meeting.) Your contact can either reach out and catch the ball, or he can deflect it, ignore it, let it fall to the ground. In either case, *you'll know what's going on.*

Don't get too excited about how well your first appointment goes. The most difficult thing is getting in the second time or the third time. It's no sin to get shot down after a first appointment. (After all, as we've seen, it's relatively easy to get!) The real sin lies in *not knowing where you stand* at the end of that first appointment.

Remember, the objective of the first step is to get to the next step, and that's all you want to do in each and every case. The only thing you should say to yourself when you evaluate your prospect is, "Have I advanced my sale?" If you have not, then you are not playing ball with your prospect, nor is your prospect playing ball with you.

Recently I had a sales representative tell me a story about a visit he made to someone who occupied a very high position within the target company. This was a woman who's been working side by side with the president of this company for sixteen years. The president trusts her implicitly and works with her day in and day out. But when this sales representative asked, "Can I come back next week to visit the president of the company?" The woman said, without missing a beat, "Well, I'll tell you the truth. He's been visiting our West Coast offices, and I don't know when he's going to be back in the office. Why don't you let me call you about how we want to proceed with this."

They've been sitting across the same desk for sixteen years. Don't you think that she knows when he's coming back from his trip to the West Coast? Of course she does. What she's done is chosen not to play ball. How do you respond to something like that? Well, you can either write a letter and follow up with a phone call asking your contact to review your preliminary outline, or you can have your manager call up a week or so later, so that manager can say, "Gee, did Jim do something wrong? I really think it would benefit everyone if he was able to sit down and talk to the president." Whatever you do, you should try to move the process forward—not leave the appointment in limbo. And if nothing happens after two or three attempts to move to the next phase, you should accept that you're not dealing with an active prospect and move on to some new opportunity.

Successful salespeople know that you have to have the prospect involved in your sale. You simply cannot sell by yourself. The prospect needs to work with you, and you have to take action at appropriate points to help move the sales process forward. What's more, when your prospect bails out, you need to be aware of that!

Understand the Underlying Purposes of the Stories You Hear

All of us communicate in stories. When somebody tells you a story, that person is actually telling you the reason he or she is doing something. I have a very good friend who spent the better part of his distinguished academic career examining the question of what motivates people to share stories with one another. He realized a long time ago that all cultures tell stories, and that *the aims of those stories are as valid and as important as the content of the stories themselves.* Successful salespeople know how to determine the underlying motives and objectives that drive the stories prospects share with them.

Understand that the purpose of a story is to communicate something. The story you hear during a sales call has a purpose. It's virtually never there solely to entertain you.

When one prospect tells you a story about a late delivery problem he had with a previous vendor, he's telling you that schedule is important to him. When another prospect tells you a story about how tough her boss was on a colleague who couldn't make the budget numbers happen, she's telling you that she needs your help to find creative ways to address the pricing issue. When another prospect tells you about a quality control nightmare she had with her most recent vendor, she's letting you know that she needs you to work with your people to meet all of her company's specifications.

You'd be surprised how many salespeople lose sight of the purpose of the stories prospects happen to share with them during phone calls and face to face meetings. My view is that there are no accidental stories during meetings with prospects. If your contact is taking the time to tell you something about how the company operates, or what his or her objective is within that company, that something is worth analyzing closely. So when you hear a story from the prospect—

whether it's about a recent event in his or her professional life or an early influence on his or her career—pull out your pen and start taking notes. Jot down all the details and then ask yourself: "What's this person trying to tell me, and how can I use what I've learned to help this person do his or her job better?"

Follow Through

Great golfers learn to follow through effectively on their swing. Great salespeople learn to follow through effectively on the relationships they establish with prospects and customers. Here are some of the ways they do it.

- *They're obsessive about writing letters.* I've mentioned this earlier in the book, but I simply can't emphasize it enough. An in-person visit should always be followed by a personal note.
- *They're obsessive about making thank-you calls.* Some of the best reps I know schedule a Thank You Day, when all they do is call current customers, check in, and say, "Thanks a lot for doing business with us." (Again, this is a practice we've adopted in my office.) Although

these calls often result in new business, they're *not* sales calls per se. They're relationship calls.

- *They find ways to help people no matter what it is, even if they don't make a sale.* My real philosophy about selling is to help people do what they do better, no matter what. What matters to me is that I'm actually able to help you. I believe that if you help enough people, for a long enough period of time, the dollars will take care of themselves. That's my philosophy, and it has helped me to build a successful sales organization. I think it's a great philosophy for any salesperson, even though it means being brave enough to say, "Hey, I don't think we can help you this time around." Simply look out for the customer or your prospect. If you're looking out for their benefit, even if you don't necessarily get an order this time around, you're eventually going to get a referral. And (what's even more important) you'll be able to sleep at night.

- *They build systems that make follow-through second nature.* As a matter of course in our company, when you become a client of ours, we send what's known as a "service letter." This is a letter from the woman who does the actual coordination of the program; she uses the note to introduce herself. But what the letter really says is, "Thank you for allowing us to be part of your training agenda. We appreciate that." We get tremendous positive reaction to that letter. The client now knows whom to contact in case there's any problem or any concern, and also knows that we value the relationship. I believe we've developed and maintained many, many long-term relationships with our clients because of that system.

Follow-through is crucial to your success. It means setting high expectations with your prospect on every single visit and call, and then living up to those expectations... time after time after time.

STRATEGY #18

Develop Disciplined, Flexible Planning Skills

Successful salespeople develop a work routine and a work ethic that allows them to execute the things they need to do each and every day. The very best use a prospect management system that allows them to rank, by basic probability, the likelihood of a sale. This system determines their schedule; it tells them exactly what they need to do on a daily basis.

The plan for the daily routine should be driven by prospecting, because, as we've seen earlier in this book, prospects have a way of evaporating while we're not looking. Let's take a look now at exactly how that happens.

Say you have twenty prospects, and your closing ratio is one in five. You make one sale, and actually loses a total of five prospects. One person becomes a customer and the others are no longer valid. You've actually lost five. Yet the typical salesperson will say to himself, "Well, I made one sale. That means I have nineteen prospects to go." No. You only have fifteen!

Then most salespeople go out and take that fifteen, thinking that they are really nineteen, and make another sale. Now they've made two sales and they think that they have eighteen prospects left, but in fact they only have ten, because they've lost—or will soon lose—ten prospects in making those two sales.

To put it bluntly: You can't ease up on prospecting once you've made a sale. After you close a sale, it's more essential than ever that you replenish your supply of prospects. So your daily activity plan *has to be driven by prospecting.*

Write this down on a card and post it somewhere where you can see it every day: "I need to prospect on a regular basis, and that should be the key to my plan."

Take a look at the number of prospects you have now that you think are almost ready to close. You need to see these people just once or twice more; you're going to have their business, and you know that. In fact, you're willing to bet money on that. My guess is there's not much more to do on those prospects, yet, if you're like most reps, you're spending proportionally more time worrying about these people than you will about developing those that are in the early stages of the game. Plan your day around those prospects with whom you're building new relationships.

Successful salespeople commit to prospecting every day—or something very close to it. That's where they know their time first needs to be spent.

When you plan out your agenda for your day, you should ask yourself: How much time should I allot for prospecting? Not servicing. Not making calls to existing accounts. Not making calls to people who are going to close. Not confirming appointments. All those tasks may be important, but they're not *as* important as prospecting. That should be first on your list.

I'm talking about making a commitment to develop brand new appointments each and every day you show up for work. I'm talking about prospecting, typically for an hour or so, and typically at the beginning of the day. Even if you say to me, "But my job is to sell to existing accounts," I've got a question for you: When was the last time you sat down and prospected an existing account—tried to find new business within an account that's already buying from you?

Salespeople who plan their day around prospecting are, by and large, successful salespeople. So that has to be your number one priority.

Life is fluid. Unexpected things are going to happen to you all the time. Therefore, you need to be ready to take a flexible approach to your goals. It's all right to adapt to new situations. In fact, it's essential. But you need to be disciplined. You need to develop a routine that's flexible and predictable enough to help you move toward your goals, day by day. You need to have the discipline to do the job each and every day.

A friend of mine is a sales representative for a major security company. He tells me each and every day is different for him. I get nervous when I hear that from a salesperson; I start worrying about how much money he's not making that he should be making. Sometimes this friend of mine gets up late. Sometimes he gets up early. Some days he makes calls. Some days he doesn't. In fact, some days, he doesn't really do much of anything.

My day, on the other hand, like the days of the superior salespeople I've worked with, is pretty much the same. I'm in the office by seven. I go home about 6:30. I work out four nights a week. I make prospect calls each and every day if I'm not training. I have slots open for meetings. I have a consistency to my training, my pacing. I've learned how to maximize my energy level; I take advantage of the rhythms of my day.

Take the same kind of approach to your sales work. Set up a basic plan for your day, a plan that allows you to count on some things (like prospecting and visiting clients) and that also lets you improvise your way through new situations that may arise.

We have a saying around my office: Obsession Without Discipline Results in Chaos. We've all seen people who are running around obsessed, determined to be successful. They're running around seven days a week twenty-four hours a day, but they never seem to get to where they're going. They never get to where they're going because they're not disciplined enough to do the right work in the first place.

Build the discipline to do the job on a continuous basis. Without the discipline, you're not going to be successful.

I think there are three key words in planning: obsession, utilization, and implementation. Yes, you've got to be obsessed. But remember that obsession without discipline results in chaos. You've got utilize all the tools and strategies available to you. And finally, you've got to get out and do it. You can't fall into the trap of planning forever and never getting around to executing the plan!

Look at the Lights of Two Cars Ahead

The other day I was driving on the Long Island Expressway and something awful almost happened. I was able to avert an accident because I was looking, not at the car in front of me, but at the car two cars in front of me. I saw those lights go on first, and I stopped in time to avoid slamming into someone.

That's the kind of thinking that's necessary for long-term success in sales. One of the big differences between successful salespeople and salespeople who don't succeed is that successful salespeople are better able to anticipate what's going to happen in the industries they sell to. They understand what's going on in the worlds that affect the worlds their customers live and work in.

You can anticipate and prepare for the obstacles your prospects and customers face. You can read the journals and industry publications that affect key industries in your prospect and customer base. You can develop networks that keep you fully informed. That means you can anticipate the responses you're likely to get. Successful salespeople learn to anticipate the objections or responses of their prospects, and they learn to prepare themselves and their organizations. They ask themselves, "What can I anticipate? What trends are emerging in industries that affect this industry? What's going to happen two car lengths ahead of me?"

When was the last time you revised your sales materials, based on new information you received from an industry trade magazine, a discussion with a key contact, or an update from the Internet? Sure, your company gives you materials, but there's no law preventing you from setting up revised versions or updating copy. And there's certainly no law preventing you from changing the questions you ask or the order in which you ask them.

The successful salesperson stays informed and constantly updates his or her anticipated sales dialogues and materials as a result of what he's learned. The successful salesperson *doesn't* wait for change to happen, but rather anticipates change and makes a habit of looking two cars ahead.

Ask, "Does this Make Sense?"

Many sales trainers will tell you never to ask a question to which the prospect could respond negatively or use as a platform to express dissatisfaction with where we're going in the interview. I think that's a load of garbage.

I've already spoken in this book about the importance of being able to ask your customer for help. (In my experience, the number one way successful salespeople do that is by being willing to say, "Hey, I must have done something wrong here. I'm sorry, please let me know where I slipped up.") What I'm asking you to look at now is the superior salesperson's willingness to ask questions that monitor where the sale is going *before* there are problems like missed appointments, flubbed presentations, and sudden, mysterious consultations with committees you didn't know existed. By asking the right "How am I doing?" questions as the sale progresses, and by physically writing down the answers you receive, you can substantially increase the likelihood that you'll stay on the right track with your prospect.

Let's say you're out driving, and you're not sure how to get to your destination. If you pull in to a gas station, roll down the window of your car, and ask the attendant how to get to West Bumbleton, there's a very good chance you're going to get one of those answers that isn't an answer at all. I don't know what your experience is in that situation, but my experience is that I'm very likely to hear something like this: "West Bumbleton, eh? Well, there are a lot of ways you could do that."

Well, you're in a hurry. You don't want to know a lot of ways. You just want to find out the best, quickest way to get to West Bumbleton. What I've learned to do helps the gas station attendant focus in a little more clearly. I say, "Listen. I've got a wedding to get to. Can you help me out? I want to get to West Bumbleton. Is it this way (pointing to the left) or is it that way (pointing to the right)?" And invariably the attendant says something like, "No, no. It's that way (pointing straight ahead)."

In a similar way, at various points in your discussion with a prospect, you're going to let the prospect correct you by presenting a couple of hypothetical options—assumptions you want to test by letting the prospect be right. (Remember, when the prospect corrects you, everyone wins!)

"So, can I assume your customers use standard-sized widgets to get their job done, or do they prefer the extra-large variety?" "Actually, most of our customers use very small widgets." "Oh, okay, small widgets." And you write "small widgets" down in your notebook. (By the way, I can't overemphasize the importance of taking good notes throughout your meetings with prospects. It gives you the information you need, encourages the prospect to open up, and raises the status of the prospect you're interviewing.)

Prospects and customers love to correct salespeople. So let them—and encourage them to do so throughout the sales process.*

---

* I should note, however, that the "hypothetical option" technique for interviewing should not be confused with the classic (and confrontational) "presumptive close." ("Do you want delivery in March or April?") I advocate the former, but not the latter.

Another, perhaps more direct way to put this principle into action is simply to say, "Am I right about so-and-so? Does this make sense?" That kind of question is likely to get you both a reaction and some new information.

"So, Mr. Smith, does what I'm talking about make sense?" Don't save that question for the closing phase! Ask it before you put together your preliminary proposal. If what you're talking about doesn't make sense to your prospect, then you can ask, "Okay, why not? Where did I take a wrong turn?" And, nine times out of ten, your prospect will say, "It's nothing you did, Jack. Here's what the problem is . . ."

Be ready, willing, and able to ask some variation on "Does this make sense?" throughout the sales cycle. Then carefully record the answers you receive.

Put the Prospect's Interests First

I honestly enjoy doing what I do. After all these years of selling and speaking—and I've spoken before 9,000 groups now—I still have a blast doing my job. I have a sincere interest in knowing about what people do and why they do it, and I think that comes through to the people I work with and the prospects and customers I interact with every day. I want to find out how I can help people do what they do better.

I don't think it's any accident that salespeople who experience high levels of success in their careers generally don't have to fake it through their discussions with customers and prospects. The stereotype of the salesperson may be the fast-talking used car salesman who manipulates people, but the reality is that people who do well in this profession don't come across as being eager to take advantage of anyone. They simply have a blast doing what they do for a living, and they genuinely enjoy talking about the pluses and the minuses of what they sell. They're sincere. They can be trusted.

The word sincere comes from the Greek derivative of "without wax." Centuries ago, when a clay pot was broken, the owner would repair the vessel with wax and keep on using it. The pot was usable, but it wasn't perfect. A really valuable pot was without wax; in other words, it was still perfect. To be a successful salesperson today, I think you must need to make sure your positive values support your actions seamlessly—that there's no wax, no gap, between what you say and what you do.

I've had situations where I had to step back from a situation and tell a prospect or customer, "Wait a minute. What's your objective here? What are you trying to get accomplished in such-and-such an area?" And the answer I received led me to believe that what the organization was after wasn't sales training or motivational training, but advanced management training work that we simply didn't offer at that time. I lost the sale—for a while—because I was honest about what my company could and couldn't do. But I kept an alliance. And I kept my integrity.

I always tell my salespeople that I would rather see them lose a sale because they were sincerely interested in the person's long-term interests than win a sale that subverts those interests. If they come to realize that this was the wrong product or service for them, it's better to be honest and to walk away than to make a sale that really does not help the prospect. That's what top-notch salespeople do, in my experience. They have enough experience, and enough integrity, to say, "You know what? I really don't think this is right for you. I think you're looking for such-and-such, and unfortunately, we don't offer that. But I can point you toward someone who does."

You have to have an underlying belief and sincerity in what you're saying in order to be successful. If you don't believe in what your organization is offering to consumers, then you should go find somewhere else to work. If you don't believe in your ability to find the best answers for your prospects and customers, or you can't tell them the truth throughout the process, then you shouldn't be in sales!

Put the prospect's interests first. You'll never regret doing so.

STRATEGY #22

Work with Prospects and Customers to Develop New Applications

Successful salespeople work with their prospects and customers to develop creative *new* answers to the questions "What do you do?" and "How can we help you do it better?" (Please remember that this is *not* the same thing as asking, "Don't you want to save money by using our widgets?")

A story I tell during training programs shows how that final question can develop naturally during the interview phase. A museum was unable to get its insurance for precious works of art to kick in during a critical period of time—the period after paintings on loan had arrived at the museum's central facility but before the assessor could inspect and catalogue them.

A sales rep for an instant camera company made a multiple-unit sale to the facility, but she didn't do it by asking "Why don't you use instant cameras in your operations?" Nobody at the museum had *thought* about using instant cameras, so she wouldn't have gotten a constructive response by asking a question like that. She found out during an interview about the particular objective of a particular decision-maker to make those dangerous three- to four-day lags between arrival and insurance coverage go away. Then, based on her thoughtful, open-minded discussions with her contact, she made a proposal. "Based on what you've told me here today, it sounds like you might be able to use a couple of our instant cameras to catalogue your recent arrivals. You could overnight the photos and logs to your insurance carrier, save their representative a trip, and get your coverage in place within forty-eight hours. That's what a lot of the other museums we've worked with have found makes sense."

It worked! But it wouldn't have if the rep hadn't found out what the museums did before launching into a preprogrammed spiel. The same goes for you. The more you find out about each and every area of a prospect's business that has some possible connection to what they sell, the more likely they are to find a new selling possibility.

Successful salespeople never stop asking:

What does the person do?
How does he or she do it?
When does he or she do it?
Where does he or she do it?
Why does he or she do it that way?
How can I help him or her do it better?

And they never stop thinking of ways they can turn the answers to those questions into new applications and solutions.

Use Fallbacks

A while back, I found myself in Dallas, Texas, working with a high-tech company. I was looking at notes that detailed people whom the company's sales representatives had called without making a sale. I went through page after page of notes, and I kept noticing that, for the most part, the space labeled "Comments" read simply "Did not buy." So I started to inquire a little bit further. I tracked down some of the salespeople who had filled out the sheets, and I asked, "Mr. Smith here, we've got him marked down as 'Did not buy,' *Why* didn't he buy?"

For the most part, there was no real reason why any given prospect didn't buy. All I would hear was, "He wasn't interested." Then I'd ask the rep what the company's focus was—what it did during the course of the average day, how it kept its customers happy and its competitors baffled—and reps often had no idea!

These lists of literally thousands of "no interest" companies were in fact particularly promising "fallback" opportunities—rejects from weeks or months past that were definitely worth another call now. I know because I called that list of "no" answers myself, and I closed 10 percent of the people on the list!

Part of the reason the prospects I spoke with were more responsive to me than they had been to the earlier reps was that I did a little bit better job of interviewing than the other people had. (For instance, I asked questions like, "How are you handling such-and-such now?" and "I'm just curious, why didn't you buy from us last time around?") But that wasn't the *whole* reason I was able to sell to that group. The truth is, *rejects don't stay rejects forever*. Time passes. People leave jobs or get promoted. Competitive challenges shift.

You and I can increase our sales totals by five to ten percent simply by using the so-called rejects I prefer to call fallbacks. When we hear a "no" from a prospect, it often means only that the prospect has decided not to buy from us right now—not that the prospect has decided not to buy anything, ever, from anyone, at any time. For example, if your prospect's company cannot exist without widgets, they're buying those widgets from some supplier. It may not be you, but they're buying from somebody. If you're a long-distance seller, the prospects you deal with are almost certainly buying long-distance from *somebody*; it just may not be you. So when you hear "No, we're not interested," what that may really mean is, "We're pretty happy with what we've got right now, and we haven't experienced any catastrophes with it recently, so we don't feel like talking to you right now." Who's to say things won't have changed four or five weeks after your call?

After a sufficient amount of time, let's say, for the sake of argument, three months, call your "old" prospects back and find out whether the same person you spoke with last time is still in charge of buying what your company sells. If you reach the same contact, say something like the following: "Listen, I understand you didn't buy from us six months ago, but I'm just calling today to find out how things are going in your widget acquisition department, and to see if you have any new projects up and running." If the contact has changed, you can start over with the new person.

Now, you're not going make every sale. But by using your fallbacks, you're going to find that you'll increase your revenue totals significantly. As I say, my experience in working with salespeople who use this strategy is that they can expect to do between five and ten percent more business.

You'll recall that earlier in this book, I recommended that you understand when to retreat. Once you've retreated for a few weeks, you should understand when an advance is in order! Don't just let your prospects sit dormant forever! Go back and check on the status of the industry, of the organization, of your contact. A year or so ago I went out on an appointment to meet with a gentleman named Alan who worked at a major oil company in California. I sat down with Alan and had a very good meeting with him, but a few weeks later, I found that, despite several attempts to reconnect on my part, Alan would not return my calls. I retreated from the sale, but a month or so later, as part of my routine of calling fallbacks, I called him up and left a dramatic message: "Alan, would you please call me. I just want to apologize for what I've done." (You'll remember that earlier in the book we examined how effective it can be to take full responsibility for the sales process. That's exactly what I did.)

Alan called me back not twenty minutes later and said, "Steve, you don't have to apologize. I've been promoted. I'm no longer in that position and I haven't been checking my voice mail on that extension. Here's the name and the number of the new person you need to talk to. Tell him I said he should get together with you." In other words, because I revisited a dormant account, there was a different situation and, eventually, some new business for my company.

Too many salespeople assume that a prospect who says no (or doesn't say anything) has dropped off the radar screen forever. It's not true! Successful salespeople revisit their fallback prospects on a regular basis—a schedule that makes sense based on the industry they work in and the customers they serve. That's not the same thing as calling back every two days and making the receptionists feel queasy when they hear your company's name! Intelligent use of fallbacks means assuming that "no" means "no for now," and scheduling a time for an intelligent status check call at a later point. Then they call back.

You can get creative when it comes to calling fallback opportunities. I've worked with reps who've gotten great results by saying, "You know, Mr. Jones, we were having a sales meeting and your name came up and I was thinking that you and I haven't talked in a while." Or if they have to leave a message, they'll simply give their number and say, "Please tell Mr. Smith I was just thinking about him and wanted to talk to him for a moment."

Try it yourself. You may be surprised at how well fallback prospects react to that simple statement: "I was just thinking about you."

Prospect Effectively

There are four steps to the appointment making process that takes place during a cold calling (or prospecting) call. The first is the opening, the second is response the person gives you, the third is the turnaround that you're going to come up with, and the fourth is actually setting the appointment. The problem is that most salespeople spend an inordinate amount of time worrying about what they are going to say in the opening. They think that if they can find a nifty grabber of an opening statement, they can forget about the work in the other three steps. The reality is that sales doesn't work that way.

Of course, you do have to begin with a compelling opening statement that sounds (and is) intelligent. It can't sound phony or unrealistic. Most salespeople start off with a statement that sounds something like this: "Good morning Mr. Jones. This is Mary Smith. The reason I'm calling you is so I can talk to you about the strategies I have for saving you a million dollars by next Monday morning." In other words, they incorporate claims that are so ludicrously exaggerated that they turn the prospect off almost immediately. (Would you believe someone who said something like that to you before they knew anything about what you do?)

A better statement might be about work that you've done successfully for somebody else. So a typical cold call from one of my top salespeople would open with something like the following: "Good morning Mr. Jones. This is Mary Smith from D.E.I. Sales Training. The reason I'm calling you today is that a couple of months ago, I finished working with the XYZ company, and I put together a program that increased their sales by 42 percent this quarter over last year. What I'd like to do is stop by next Tuesday at three and simply tell you about the success I've had for them."

What you do by using that kind of statement is to create a meaningful basis for a conversation based *not* on what you can do for the prospect (about whom you now know little or nothing), but on what you've done for someone else. That's a realistic foundation for future discussions.

What happens next? Should you expect the prospect to start asking questions about your work with XYZ, or congratulating you on the great results you were able to deliver? Well, that's nice when it happens, but you should probably be ready for some other outcomes, too. The prospect is going to respond to you, and that response shouldn't take you by surprise.

The most successful sales reps know that the responses that arise out of a statement like the one you just read are usually going to have some connection to what the prospect does. Not what you do, but what the prospect does: "We don't do sales training." "We handle all that in house." "We don't use trainers we haven't worked with before." "We just have absolutely no interest." A superior salesperson is going to effectively turn that response around by saying something like this: "You know, Mr. Smith, that's exactly what a lot of my customers said to me before they saw how our programs could complement their existing training programs. What kind of in-house programs are you conducting now?" In other words, you use their response to focus in on one of the questions about what the prospect's company is doing right now.

After you listen carefully and jot down the information you receive, you're going to repeat your request for an appointment: "You know, Mr. Smith, based on what you've told me during this call, I really think we ought to get together to talk about this in person. How's Tuesday at three?" Sometimes, thank goodness, you'll hear the prospect say, "Okay. Tuesday sounds good."

If you conduct your prospecting calls in the way I've laid them out above, and you do it consistently—devoting perhaps an hour every day to the process—then you'll get the appointments you need. No doubt about it.

As I've mentioned, I prospect on a regular basis, and so do my own salespeople. Each and every day that I'm not in front of a group, I will pick up the phone and make fifteen calls. I get through to seven people and set up one new appointment a day. I do this five days a week, so I'm averaging five new appointments a week. My closing ratio is one out of eight; for every eight appointments I make a sale.* I bring in fifty new accounts a year. Those are my numbers. What are yours?

---

* I average eight total appointments per week; five new appointments and three to follow through on past visits.

Prospecting makes all those ratios happen. It's the activity that gets the whole process started. If you skip it, or wait until your current business dries up, then you're riding for a fall. If you make a commitment to do a little bit of prospecting every day, then the first part of your ratio is in place. Then you can look at every other link in the chain and ask yourself, "What needs improving? What would happen if I scheduled one more appointment per week? How would that affect the whole structure? Or perhaps I could improve my interviewing and develop better presentations. If I worked more closely with prospects, found a way to tailor my presentations more to their situations, could I close one more sale per month as a result?"

Prospect every day—and keep an eye on your numbers. Where appropriate, set new targets for yourself. Develop a set of targets that makes sense for your industry and your income goals and then commit to the front end of your sales cycle by making the calls you need to make, day after day, no matter what.

Keep the Closing Phase Simple

"My boss is going to fire me if you don't sign this contract."

"Here's a pen. Here's a contract. Press hard, you're making three copies."

"Let's play a game. You write down all the reasons you think you shouldn't buy our widgets, and if I come up with reasons that prove yours don't matter, I win, and you have to buy from us."

"Did you want the green widgets or the blue widgets?"

"Let me leave the unit here with you for a week. I'm so sure you'll fall in love with it, I'm willing to bet you'll sign up with us after you see what it can do for your operation."

"If you buy from me today, I'll win a trip to Hawaii. My family's really counting on that vacation."

All these closing "tricks" (I won't call them strategies) share a distinct disadvantage. They each attempt to dictate terms to the prospect, to make the purchase decision for him or her, to manipulate the prospect into buying. Although you'll still find some sales managers praising these ancient tricks to the heavens (I even came across one trainer in Florida who claimed to have invented a few!), you won't find superior salespeople using them.

The best salespeople have a very simple, very powerful two-phase strategy for initiating new business with their contacts. First, they actively solicit all the objections they possibly can before the close, typically by encouraging prospects to rewrite preliminary versions of their formal presentations. Then, after all the important players in the target organization have signed off on all the key elements of the initial proposal (or "pre-proposal," as we call it in our office), successful salespeople deliver a flawless formal presentation that concludes with the showstopper closing technique to beat all showstopper closing techniques.

They say, "So, Mr. Smith, that's our proposal. I have to tell you, we've spent a lot of time putting this together, and it really makes sense to me. Does it make sense to you?"

That's the closing technique that I've taught top salespeople all over the country to use. I use it myself. If I understand fully what the prospect does, and if my program honestly makes sense to me after I've worked hard during the interviewing phase to uncover exactly what it is they do and how I can help them do it better, "You know Mr. Prospect, this plan really makes sense to me."

Now only two things can happen at that point. Mr. Smith is either going to say, "Yes, it makes sense to me, too," in which case I've got a sale, or he's going to say "No, it doesn't make sense to me, Steve." If it doesn't make sense to Mr. Smith, then I don't know as much about the company as I thought I did. (Remember that successful salespeople only close *after* they've achieved full buy-in on all pertinent aspects of the preliminary plan. If you don't have "go" signals from your decision-makers at the end of your preliminary proposal, you're not ready for a formal proposal yet!)

If Mr. Smith says, "No, this doesn't really make sense," I can pull back and allow myself to be corrected and say, "Well, gee, I must have taken a wrong turn somewhere. I'm sorry. Where did I go wrong in my plan? What doesn't make sense?" Then I take detailed notes on everything that Mr. Smith says (which is something I should have been doing long before I attempted to close the sale).

Closing the sale isn't a matter of spouting a series of magic words that you hope against hope will somehow trick the prospect into buying from you. It's the natural outcome of an extended process during which you listen to what the prospect has to say and propose creative, customized ways he or she can begin to use what you have to offer.

Closing cannot happen if you haven't yet found out what the prospect does! So find out what the prospect does. Take all the time you can to do so. Develop a good plan, one that takes full advantage of the prospect's knowledge and insights. Make sure it's a customized plan, one that is tailored to what your prospect is trying to get done. Then, and only then, you should be ready to say, "It makes sense to me. What do you think?"

Will *some* people buy from you if you trick them into thinking that your kids will go hungry next week if you don't bring a signed contract back to the office? Will *some* people buy from you if you manipulate them or play head games? Will *some* people buy from you simply because you represent a short-term solution to a short-term problem—and they're willing to overlook shameless closing ploys (for now)? Sure. But you won't sell as much as you deserve to, and your customers won't stick with you over time. They certainly won't become partners with you and your organization.

Mediocre salespeople use mediocre techniques, and they achieve consistently mediocre results. Successful salespeople recognize that the foundation for all solid business relationships is trust. They know that they have to earn the trust of their prospects by learning all they possibly can about them, and by only making suggestions that they truly feel are in the prospect's best interest. That doesn't mean they close every sale, but it does mean that every new piece of business they bring in carries the seeds of a mutually beneficial partnership. And when you think about it, that's the very best way to start out new relationships and reinforce existing ones.

May you always be ready to ask the right questions and may the right doors always open for you as you pursue your sales career. Good luck!

About the Author

Stephan Schiffman has trained over 250,000 salespeople at firms such as AT&T Information Systems, Chemical Bank, Manufacturers Hanover Trust, Motorola, and U.S. Healthcare. Mr. Schiffman, president of DEI Management Group, is the author of *Cold Calling Techniques (That Really Work!)*, *The 25 Most Common Sales Habits of Highly Successful Salespeople*, and a number of other popular books on sales.

Do you have questions, comments, or suggestions regarding this book? Please share them with me! Write to me at this address: *sschiffman@steveschiffman.com*.